Mexico

Beth Gruber

Gary S. Elbow, Ph.D., and Jorge Zamora, Ph.D., Consultants

NATIONAL GEOGRAPHIC

WASHINGTON, D.C.

Contents

MODERN MEXICO is the product of a rich Indian heritage, three centuries of Spanish rule, and a shared border with the world's richest country—the United States.

Mexicans take great pride in the Olmec, Maya, Aztec, and other ancient Indian cultures that created some of the world's most advanced civilizations. The Spanish conquest in 1521 ended Indian rule here but not the influence of its traditions. Today, most Mexicans are mestizos—a mix of Spanish and Indian blood. Everything from religious celebrations to handicrafts reflects a blend of Spanish and native culture.

Mexicans also remember that as part of Spain's empire in the New World, the borders of their country once extended as far north as Wyoming, as far west as California, and as far east as Louisiana. Today, many Americans express concern about the number of Mexicans who cross the border legally and illegally. But the truth is that much of the American West has been the homeland of Mexicans for many generations.

The Mexico–United States border is the sharpest economic divide in the world. South of it nearly 40 percent of Mexico's people live in poverty. For many, the best chance for a better life lies in migrating to the U.S. The huge increase in Mexican immigrants—hundreds of thousands each year—has spurred efforts to integrate the economies of the two countries. The most recent step in this process was the enactment of NAFTA (North American Free Trade Agreement) in 1994. Although NAFTA has greatly increased trade between the United States and Mexico, it is still too soon to tell what the long-range impact on Mexico's economy will be. The hope is that NAFTA, by increasing trade and industrialization, will reduce unemployment and increase wages for Mexican workers. If the country's

economy grows as a result of NAFTA, Mexico could serve as a model for other countries in Latin America and the world.

This book is designed to provide a comprehensive picture of Mexico—its geography, environment, history, culture, politics, and economy—that will help readers understand what makes it one of the world's most interesting and important countries. What happens in Mexico may well affect the pattern of future development in other emerging countries.

▲ These cowboys are among those Mexicans who choose to work in the United States, where wages are higher.

Gary Elbow

Gary S. Elbow, Ph.D.
Professor of Geography
Honors College
Texas Tech University

Land of *Extremes*

ON A CLEAR DAY, people in Mexico City can see a huge snowcapped volcano towering in the distance. Known as El Popo—short for Popocatépetl (poh-poh-ka-TAY-pet-ul), or "smoking mountain"—it stands almost 18,000 feet (5,500 m) high and often blows off steam. More than 19 million people live within 50 miles (80 km) of El Popo; but for nearby farmers, it is a blessing. The volcanic soil is fertile, and storm clouds gather along its slopes, producing rainfall.

This is a land of extremes, with high mountains, deep canyons, sweeping deserts, and dense rain forests. To study Mexico's geography is to explore the impact of this rugged, beautiful land on the Mexican people and their culture.

◀ The steaming crater of Popocatépetl looms above a church, which stands on a mound that may have been built to honor El Popo.

WHAT'S THE WEATHER LIKE?

Mexico's climate is ruled by the land's elevation and influenced by the oceans.

Roughly two-thirds of Mexico lies south of the Tropic of Cancer (the imaginary line where the sun passes directly overhead at noon on the first day of summer). Low-lying areas in the south have tropical weather. Places at higher elevations are cooler. Most rain falls between May and October. The map opposite shows the physical features of Mexico. Labels on this map and on similar maps throughout this book identify places pictured in each chapter.

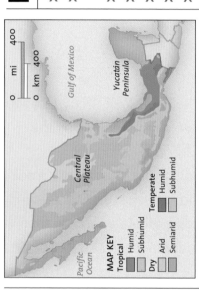

Pacific Ocean

Gulf of Mexico

Central Plateau

Yucatán Peninsula

0 mi 400
0 km 400

MAP KEY
Tropical
Humid
Subhumid
Dry
Arid
Semiarid
Temperate
Humid
Subhumid

Average Temperature & Rainfall

Average High/Low Temperatures; Yearly Rainfall

North Pacific coast:
86° F (30° C) / 64° F (17° C); 6 in (17 cm)

Northwest interior:
78° F (25° C) / 56° F (13° C); 9 in (23 cm)

South Pacific coast:
88° F (31° C) / 75° F (23° C); 18 in (44 cm)

Central Plateau:
74° F (23° C) / 52° F (11° C); 25 in (63 cm)

East coast:
86° F (30° C) / 67° F (19° C); 22 in (58 cm)

Yucatán Peninsula:
90° F (32° C) / 70° F (21° C); 36 in (91 cm)

Fast Facts

> **OFFICIAL NAME:** United Mexican States

> **FORM OF GOVERNMENT:** republic of federated states

> **CAPITAL:** Mexico City

> **POPULATION:** 106,202,903

> **OFFICIAL LANGUAGE:** Spanish

> **MONETARY UNIT:** the peso

> **AREA:** 758,449 square miles (1,964,375 square kilometers)

> **BORDERING NATIONS:** United States, Guatemala, Belize

> **HIGHEST POINT:** Citlaltépetl (Volcán Pico de Orizaba) 18,855 feet (5,747 meters)

> **LOWEST POINT:** Laguna Salada in the Mexicali Valley, 35 feet (10 meters) below sea level

> **MAJOR MOUNTAIN RANGES:** Sierra Madre Oriental, Sierra Madre Occidental

> **MAJOR RIVERS:** Rio Grande (Río Bravo del Norte), Yaqui, Pánuco, Balsas, Grijalva

Atlantic
Ocean

North
America

U.S.

MEXICO

Pacific
Ocean

South
America

UNITED STATES

Gulf of Mexico

Cabo Catoche

YUCATÁN
PENINSULA

Cozumel I.

TULUM,
page 15

Chetumal
Bay

Hondo

BELIZE

TROPIC OF CANCER

Términos
Lagoon

Usumacinta

EL + Chichón
3,478 ft
1,060 m

Grijalva

GUATEMALA

Sierra Madre

HONDURAS

EL SALVADOR

Madre Lagoon

LANDSCAPE OF
GUANAJUATO,
page 1

CALLAGHAN RANCH,
page 5

Pánuco

Cabo Rojo

MEXICO CITY,
page 13

Pico de Orizaba
(Highest point in Mexico)
+ 18,855 ft
5,747 m

Isthmus of
Tehuantepec

Gulf of
Tehuantepec

Sierra Madre del Sur

Rio Grande
(Rio Bravo del Norte)

S I E R R A   M A D R E   O R I E N T A L

Central
Plateau

RIO GRANDE,
page 11

M E X I C O

Conchos

Popocatépetl +
17,802 ft
5,426 m

México ✪

Balsás

Petacalco Bay

Lerma

Lake Chapala

Rio Grande
de Santiago

Paricutín Volcano
8,989 ft +
2,740 m

Lázaro Cárdenas

San Telmo Point

EARTHQUAKE,
page 14

SIERRA MADRE OCCIDENTAL

Yaqui

Banderas Bay

HUICHOL INDIAN CHILDREN,
page 12

Cabo
San Lucas

POPOCATÉPETL VOLCANO,
pages 2, 6-7

Laguna Salada
(Lowest point
in Mexico)
-33 ft
-10 m

Altar
Desert

Sonoran

Desert

Tiburón

Gulf of California

BAJA CALIFORNIA

Cabo San Lázaro

Eugenia
Point

Pacific Ocean

MAP KEY

✪ National capital
● Selected city
+ Elevation

miles   500

0   500

kilometers

0

Rio Grande: Where Nations Meet

The Rio Grande forms the boundary between Mexico and the U.S. for nearly 1,250 miles (2,000 km). Originating high in the Rocky Mountains of Colorado, the river begins its long journey between nations at Ciudad Juárez (SEE-OO-dad WHA-rez), across from El Paso, Texas.

Near the Gulf of Mexico, farmers draw water from the Rio Grande to irrigate crops. Upstream, it runs largely through desert country, including the scenic wilderness along the Big Bend. At the Big Bend, boundaries between nations mean little. This was all Mexican country before Americans took control of the north side of the river, after defeating Mexico in 1848. Since then, millions of Mexicans have crossed the Rio Grande, seeking opportunity in the United States. As this massive migration continues, Mexicans and Americans are creating a vibrant new culture along the riverbanks.

Baja California: Desert by the Sea

▲ Peccaries, also known as javelinas, are common sights along the Rio Grande.

Extending southward from the U.S. state of California, the Baja (BAH-hah) California Peninsula is surrounded on three sides by water. But few places in Mexico are drier than Baja California, where many spots receive

less than four inches (10 cm) of rainfall a year. In 1535, Spanish conquistador Hernán Cortés came to Baja searching for treasure. Instead he found tens of thousands of Indians (native Mexican people) who survived on the barren land by eating cactus, other desert plants, and snakes, lizards, and iguanas.

Progress has come slowly to Baja California. Its first paved road was not completed until 1923. That highway will take you to coastal resorts like Ensenada, popular with sunbathers and whale watchers. But if you want to explore the interior, you must follow dirt roads.

▲ The Rio Grande separates a mountain range in the Mexican state of Chihuahua (upper left) from similar country at Big Bend Ranch State Park in Texas (foreground).

▲ Huichol Indian girls lead their burro past a cornfield in the Sierra Madre Occidental.

Be sure to carry plenty of water. Losing your way here is like being stranded on a desert island.

Treasures of the Sierra Madre

Much of Mexico is mountainous. Between the Sierra Madre Oriental (east) and the Sierra Madre Occidental (west) lie smaller mountain ranges on the Central Plateau. These mountainous regions are rich in precious ores (rock or gravel containing silver or copper), which miners can remove with picks and shovels.

When Spanish colonists first came to Mexico, they forced Indians to labor in the mines and remove the

NORTH AMERICA'S MOST DRAMATIC RAILWAY

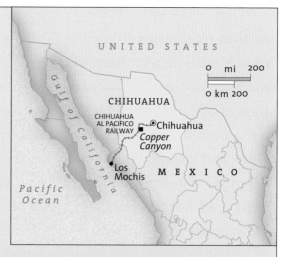

The Chihuahua al Pacífico Railway runs through the Copper Canyon where the Tarahumara make their home. Although many Tarahumara work in hotels and restaurants at stations along the way, they seldom ride the train themselves. Instead, this 415-mile (670-km)-long railway—often called North America's most dramatic railway—attracts thousands of tourists every year. They come to see more of this spectacular country, including the 87 tunnels and 36 bridges the famous train traverses on its 16-hour journey.

valuable ore. Many Indians died. Others, like the Tarahumara of Chihuahua (chee-WAH-wah), took refuge in a remote area of the Sierra Madre Occidental called Barranca del Cobre, or Copper Canyon, where cliffs rise more than a mile (1.6 km) above the Río Urique.

Like the Tarahumara, the Huichol (WEE-chol), cared little for silver or gold. To them, the real treasure of the Sierra Madre was maize, or corn, domesticated 4,000 years ago from a Mexican wild grass.

Mexico City: Living on Shaky Ground

▼ Mexico's capital is commonly called Mexico City, but its proper name is simply Mexico.

Set at an elevation of 7,296 feet (2,224 m), sprawling Mexico City is high but not dry. Much of this area was once covered by shallow Lake Texcoco. Spanish settlers drained the lake and built heavily on that soft foundation. Today, some buildings are sinking up to six inches (15 cm) a year into the spongy

lake bed. When earthquakes hit, the muck beneath Mexico City shakes like jelly, worsening the damage.

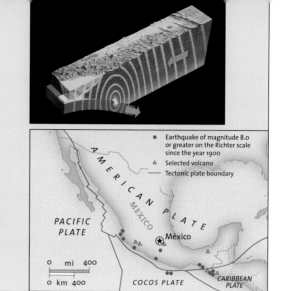

WHAT MAKES THE EARTH SHAKE?

Earthquakes are caused by friction between plates that form the Earth's crust. Along the west coast of Mexico, the Cocos Plate (see map at right) is sliding under the American Plate, causing tension to build. On September 19, 1985, the tension was released (above right), causing shock waves that rocked Mexico City.

Map labels:
- Earthquake of magnitude 8.0 or greater on the Richter scale since the year 1900
- △ Selected volcano
- Tectonic plate boundary

PACIFIC PLATE

AMERICAN PLATE

MEXICO

México

0 mi 400
0 km 400

COCOS PLATE

CARIBBEAN PLATE

▲ The earthquake that originated west of Mexico City in September 1985 mangled these railroad tracks on the Pacific Coast.

Anatomy of an Earthquake

On the morning of September 19, 1985, Mexico City was jolted by a severe earthquake that killed more than 9,000 people and destroyed hundreds of buildings. The quake, which measured 8.1 on the Richter scale, was centered some 220 miles (350 km) west of the city at a fault line where two plates in the Earth's crust grind together. The shaking and grinding at the fault line was over in about 30 seconds, but shock waves caused the spongy ground under Mexico City to quiver for three terrifying minutes.

Yucatán Peninsula: Land of the Maya

The Yucatán Peninsula at Mexico's southeastern tip was once home to Maya civilization. Maya still live in and around the Yucatán, where ancestral ruins such as

Tulum are popular tourist attractions. Near Tulum, an unspoiled area along the Gulf Coast has been set aside as a biosphere reserve. The reserve includes lobster fisheries worked by Maya, ancient canals and temples, and habitat for endangered loggerhead turtles and hundreds of bird species.

The Yucatán has tropical weather—warm throughout the year—but not all spots receive heavy amounts of rainfall. The hilly area bordering Guatemala has drenching summer downpours that support dense rain forests. Farther north on the Yucatán Peninsula, the land is flat and dry. When rain falls here, it seeps through the ground and flows freely into limestone caverns that serve as reservoirs for the local people. Once, these same caverns were sacred places, used by the ancient Maya for worship and human sacrifice.

▼ Located on the Gulf of Mexico near the tip of the Yucatán Peninsula, Tulum was an ancient Maya center of commerce.

Mexico's Living Wonders

THE FIERCE JAGUAR has long been feared and revered in Mexico. Ancient Maya believed that the setting sun turned into a jaguar and prowled the underworld until dawn. Aztec warriors called Jaguar Knights cut out captives' hearts at an altar decorated with the head of a jaguar.

Today, jaguars have lost two-thirds of their original habitat in Mexico and live mainly in forests in the south. Their talent for survival is shared by animals and plants in other challenging environments, like the deserts of northern Mexico. Many species that inhabit this country or stop here on epic migrations are living wonders—as miraculous in their own way as the fearsome jaguar that inspired the Aztec and Maya.

◀ Hunters of the night, jaguars use their deadly fangs to kill deer, javelinas, and armadillos, as well as livestock such as pigs and cattle.

A NATURAL WILDLIFE REFUGE

Located partway between the Equator and the Arctic Circle, Mexico is a refuge for species fleeing extreme cold to the north and intense heat to the south. Blessed with many different climate zones and habitats, the country supports a huge variety of plants and animals.

The map opposite shows vegetation zones—or what lives where—in Mexico. Vegetation zones form ecosystems, or environments that support specific plant and animal life. Few nations on Earth support as many different plant and animal species as Mexico.

▲ **Populations of loggerhead turtles in the Gulf of Mexico are in decline.**

Species at Risk

Human activities such as farming, logging, and hunting reduce natural habitats and threaten many of Mexico's native creatures with extinction. The following species are among those at risk:

> Chiapan climbing rat
> Resplendent quetzal
> Cozumel Island coati
> Coahuila box turtle
> Desert tortoise
> Volcano rabbit
> Flat-headed myotis bat
> Blue whale
> Guadalupe fur seal
> Mexican spotted terrapin

> Jaguar
> Loggerhead turtle
> Mexican spotted owl
> Oaxaca hummingbird
> Omiltemi rabbit
> Mexican black howler monkey
> Sonoran pronghorn
> Gila monster
> Yaqui catfish
> Imperial woodpecker

Vegetation & Ecosystems Map

UNITED STATES

Tijuana
Mexicali

Altar Desert

Sonoran Desert

Ciudad Juárez

Chihuahua

Rio Grande
(Rio Bravo del Norte)
Conchos

Yaqui

Tiburón

BAJA CALIFORNIA

Vizcaíno Desert

Gulf of California

Pacific Ocean

SIERRA MADRE OCCIDENTAL

SIERRA MADRE ORIENTAL

Cuatro Ciénegas

Monterrey

San Luis Potosí

León

Guadalajara

Acapulco

Balsas

México

Puebla

Sierra Madre del Sur

Pánuco

Tampico

Veracruz

Isthmus of Tehuantepec

Gulf of Tehuantepec

Sierra Madre

Usumacinta

Grijalba

Hondo

Mérida

YUCATÁN PENINSULA

Gulf of Mexico

TROPIC OF CANCER

BELIZE

GUATEMALA

HONDURAS

EL SALVADOR

CUATRO CIÉNEGAS NATURAL PROTECTED AREA, page 20 (top) AND MORNING GLORIES, page 23 (bottom)

COASTAL WETLAND, page 23 (top)

GRAY WHALE MIGRATION, page 22

DESERT LIFE, pages 20 (bottom), 21

miles
kilometers
0   500
0   500

MAP KEY

Primary Vegetation Zones/Ecosystems

- Arid or semiarid shrubland
- Tropical dry forest
- Tropical rain forest
- Grassland
- Temperate forest

Protected Lands

- National park
- Other protected land

Thriving in the Desert

The deserts of northern Mexico may look barren, but they are brimming with plant and animal species that have found ways to survive and thrive here. Desert plants cope not just with drought but also with desert animals that feed on them. The cactus and boojum tree, for example, have spines or thorns to discourage rodents, reptiles, or birds from gnawing at their moist stems or eating the flowers, fruits, and seeds by which they reproduce. The creosote bush produces a smelly resin that keeps creatures away. All desert plants have unique root systems that allow them to absorb water whenever rain falls and store it for long periods of time. Some cactuses can survive for more than a year on the water they absorb from a single rainstorm.

Desert animals have their own strategies for surviving heat and drought. Many rodents and snakes are

▲ Cactus flowers in bloom are shielded by spines that keep off most intruders, except hovering birds or bees, which help the plant reproduce by spreading pollen.

▼ Boojum trees grow as tall as 50 feet (15 meters) high and usually flower in late summer, the season when rain is most likely to fall.

nocturnal. They sleep during the day and come out at night. Some lizards are active in the day but scurry from one shady spot to another to keep cool. Desert toads bury themselves during drought and lie dormant until it rains, when they emerge to breed. Desert iguanas sometimes take over burrows dug by kangaroo rats. Those stolen burrows keep iguanas cool and protect them from predators, including humans, who, in some parts of Mexico, eat them for food.

▲ The tough hide of the desert iguana—an animal that feeds mainly on plants—allows it to crawl on this cactus without being hurt by the plant's protective spines.

Nurseries for Gray Whales

Every December, thousands of gray whales enter lagoons along the west coast of Baja California to mate and give birth to calves in the warm, sheltered waters. Their arrival marks the end of a strenuous 5,000-mile (8,047-km) journey from Alaskan waters, where the gray whales feed through the summer.

Only half the adult females who come to Baja are available for courtship in any one year. Outnumbered by adult males two to one, they have plenty of admirers. Naturalists studying the behavior of gray whales wintering off Baja have observed them to be highly sociable. They typically can be found frolicking together in groups of two or three cows and calves and are mindful of the youngest whales who play among them.

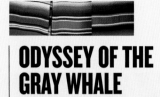

ODYSSEY OF THE GRAY WHALE

The gray whale's 5,000-mile (8,047-km) journey between its Baja California breeding ground and Alaskan feeding ground is the longest migration made by any mammal.

Beginning in late January, males leave the Baja lagoons to return to the Arctic. Pregnant females remain until April to give birth and nurse their calves, who train for the long trip to Alaska by swimming in the lagoons against strong tidal currents. Come mid-spring, they leave their Baja nurseries and head north with their mothers. One day, these same calves will return to raise their own offspring here.

▼ A gray whale breaches off the coast of Baja California.

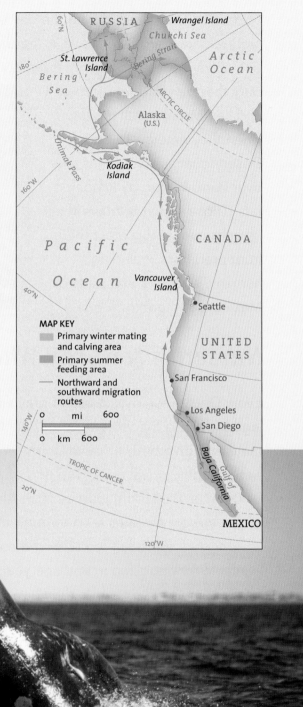

MAP KEY
- Primary winter mating and calving area
- Primary summer feeding area
- Northward and southward migration routes

Diversity in the Tropics

The quetzal—like the jaguar—has long inspired wonder and awe. Its stunning green tail feathers adorned the headdresses of Aztec rulers, who worshipped a god called Quetzalcoatl (ket-sahl-ko-wat-ul), or Feathered Serpent. In ancient times, killing a quetzal was punishable by death. Today, they are a protected species but are threatened by loss of habitat.

Preserving the rain forests where quetzals, spider monkeys, and other enchanting creatures make their home is essential. Scientists explore these rain forests for many reasons, often in the hope of finding new species that may lead to medical breakthroughs. Some tropical plants and insects contain substances that can ease pain or cure disease. Of all the living wonders in Mexico, the most miraculous may be lifesaving species that have yet to be discovered.

▲ Egrets find refuge in Mexico's rain forests and coastal wetlands.

▼ Morning glories abound in Cuatro Cienegas Natural Protected Area.

Monuments
to a
Majestic
Past

NOT FAR FROM MEXICO CITY stand the remains of Teotihuacán (tayoh-tee-wah-KAHN), one of the largest cities in the ancient world. The leaders of Teotihuacán and other cities ruled like gods and demanded sacrifices in labor, goods, and blood from their subjects. In this fashion, Maya and Aztec rulers lived in splendor for many centuries.

When Spain took control of Mexico in the 1500s, colonists created their own society, relying on the efforts of poor people at the bottom to support a privileged few at the top. Not until Mexicans rebelled against Spain in 1810 did that society begin to crumble. A bloody revolution in the early 1900s has played a very important role in the formation of present-day Mexico.

◀ The Pyramid of the Sun looms over the remains of Teotihuacán, an ancient planned city of temples, apartments, and workshops.

ANCIENT CULTURES

The Olmec people, Mexico's first complex society, emerged around 1200 B.C. By A.D. 300 the Maya had mastered the art of writing and were building cities.

Meanwhile, Teotihuacán was growing rich and strong. After it collapsed, other powers, including the warlike Toltec and the mighty Aztec, rose up nearby. In 1521, Spaniards defeated the Aztec and ruled the country for 300 years.

The historical map opposite shows areas occupied by these ancient cultures and where remains of ancient cities or ceremonial sites can be found. It also shows the route followed by Spanish conquistadores, who sailed to Mexico in 1519. If you compare this map to the modern population density map on page 39, you will see that the fertile south was the cradle of Mexican civilization and remains home to much of the population today.

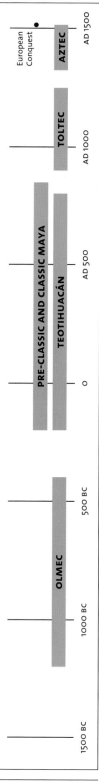

Matthew Stirling and his team uncovered Olmec masterpieces like this stone head, found at Tres Zapotes. The head weighed more than six tons (5.5 metric tons).

Time line

This chart shows the approximate dates for major cultures that developed and declined in Mexico between 1500 B.C. and A.D. 1521, when the Aztec empire fell to Spanish conquistadores (conquerors).

1500 BC	1000 BC	500 BC	0	AD 500	AD 1000	AD 1500

OLMEC

PRE-CLASSIC AND CLASSIC MAYA

TEOTIHUACÁN

TOLTEC

AZTEC

European Conquest

UNITED STATES

Ciudad Juárez

Sonoran Desert

Altar Desert

Gulf of California

BAJA CALIFORNIA

Pacific Ocean

SIERRA MADRE OCCIDENTAL

SIERRA MADRE ORIENTAL

M E X I C O

Satevó

San Juan del Rio

MISSION CHURCH, page 32

PANCHO VILLA BIRTHPLACE, page 35 (top)

Gulf of Mexico

TROPIC OF CANCER

500 miles

500 kilometers

México

Tenochtitlán

Anenecuilco

Teotihuacán

Tres Zapotes

Oaxaca

Sierra Madre del Sur

La Venta

Palenque

Bonampak

Yucatán Peninsula

BELIZE

GUATEMALA

Sierra Madre

EL SALVADOR

Cortés's route from Cuba

PYRAMID OF THE SUN, pages 2–3, 24–25

MAYA CITY-STATE, pages 29, 30 (top)

OLMEC HEAD, page 26

ARCHAEOLOGICAL DIG, page 28

AZTEC SACRIFICE, page 30 (bottom)

EMILIANO ZAPATA BIRTHPLACE, page 35 (bottom)

TURQUOISE-COVERED SKULL, page 31

MAP KEY

- Selected present-day city
- Archaeological site
- Cortés's route

Olmec heartland, 1200–400 B.C.

Maya region, A.D. 250–900

Aztec empire, A.D. 1300–1521

Overlapping area

Present-day country boundaries and place names are shown.

On Assignment: Unearthing Olmec Treasures

Archaeologists explore the past by studying the remains of people and their buildings, belongings, and works of art. In 1939, archaeologist Matthew Stirling took on a big challenge. His assignment was to excavate sites in Mexico where huge stone heads, believed to have been crafted by the Olmec in 1200 B.C., were embedded in the earth. Stirling's excavations at those sites were sponsored by the National Geographic Society and the Smithsonian Institution. His efforts

▼ **Workers with Stirling's expedition use logs to prop up a massive, intricately carved stone at La Venta.**

added greatly to our knowledge of the Olmec people, who produced the stone heads as well as other remarkable works of art.

The Magnificent Maya

In A.D. 615 a commanding figure named Pakal became ruler of the Maya kingdom of Palenque (pah-LEN-kay). He held power for 68 years and represented Maya civilization at its peak.

▲ Maya pyramids, like this one at Palenque, have stairways leading to temples at the top.

Maya city-states were often at war with each other. One reason they fought was to take captives. To avoid misfortune, rulers sacrificed captives—and sometimes even drops of their very own blood—to the gods. Before launching an attack, they consulted astronomers who studied the movements of heavenly bodies like the planet Venus, which was thought to govern warfare.

Astronomers also predicted eclipses of the sun and moon and kept a calendar that told people when to plant crops and hold ceremonies. Scribes recorded Maya history in writing. Shrewd rulers like Pakal made alliances and devoted some time to peaceful pursuits. The magnificent Palenque, at its peak during Pakal's reign, displayed the skills of Maya artists and architects.

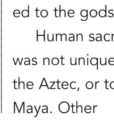
Aztec Splendor and Sacrifice

The power of the Aztec empire was symbolized by the Great Pyramid. It stood at the center of the Aztec capital of Tenochtitlán (tay-noch-teet-LAHN), which was founded in the early 1300s at what is now Mexico City.

On important occasions, captives were sacrificed by the thousands atop the Great Pyramid at temples dedicated to the gods.

Human sacrifice was not unique to the Aztec, or to the Maya. Other

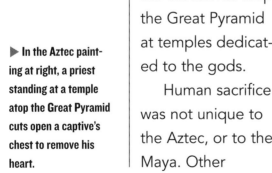

Mexican societies practiced it, as did ancient Romans in Europe, whose gladiator contests originated at funerals as blood offerings to the dead. Like the Romans, the Aztec combined cruelty with great accomplishments. Aztec priests were scholars who wrote books, observed the heavens, and kept a calendar much like the one used by the Maya. Tenochtitlán itself was a sophisticated seat of government, divided into nearly 80 districts, each of which had its own council and school and provided up to 400 soldiers in time of war.

The Spanish Conquest

Spanish exploration of the New World began in 1492, when Christopher Columbus crossed the Atlantic and claimed Cuba and other Caribbean islands for Spain. In 1519, Hernán Cortés sailed from Cuba to Mexico's Gulf coast and marched inland to Tenochtitlán, a city larger than any in Spain.

The Aztec emperor Moctezuma welcomed Cortés, who pretended to have peaceful intentions. Soon after, Cortés took Moctezuma prisoner while he was visiting the Spaniards. The capture cost Moctezuma his honor, and he was killed by his own people during an attack on Cortés, who escaped. In 1521, while the Aztec were plagued by smallpox and other diseases introduced by Spaniards, Cortés and his allies seized and destroyed their capital. From the ruins rose the Spanish colonial capital of Mexico City.

▲ This turquoise-covered skull may be the head of a man who played the part of the supreme Aztec god and was treated with great respect before he was sacrificed.

From Spanish Colony to Nation

Spaniards who colonized Mexico replaced the Aztec pyramids with majestic Catholic churches and cathedrals. As before, the task of building those monuments required by Mexico's new rulers fell to people under their power.

In 1542 Spain outlawed the enslavement of Indians, but colonists in Mexico found other ways of forcing natives to labor for them. Some Indians toiled on estates called haciendas for wages so low, they were not much better off than slaves. Others worked as vaqueros (cowboys) on ranches, overseeing horses, cattle, and other animals imported from Spain.

▼ Mission churches like this one at Satevó in Mexico's Copper Canyon were built by Indians.

MEXICO LOSES GROUND

Mexico lost more than half the territory it inherited from Spain in 1821—a vast area stretching from Central America to what is now the American West. Central American lands seceded in 1823. Texas broke free in 1836 and became part of the U.S. in 1846.

That led to the Mexican-American War in 1846. Invaded and defeated, Mexico gave up California, New Mexico, and other territory in 1848. The U.S. acquired more land from Mexico for cash in 1853, leaving the border where it stands today.

MAP KEY
- Mexico in 1821
- Territory lost, 1823
- Territory lost, 1836–1845
- Territory lost, 1848
- Territory sold, 1853
- Present-day Mexico
- Present-day international boundaries
- Present-day U.S. state boundaries

By 1800, most Mexicans were tired of being treated like subjects. In 1810 a Catholic priest named Miguel Hidalgo y Costilla, who was influenced by the ideas of the French and American Revolutions, spoke out for the people and launched a rebellion against Spain that ended in 1821 when Mexico won independence.

A Troubled Young Nation

In 1824 Mexicans adopted a constitution that gave more power to the nation's states than to the central government. It was a radical change for a country accustomed to being ruled by royalty. Before long, dictators backed by the army seized power again and threw out the new constitution. But their government was weak and eventually lost vast territory to the U.S. during the Mexican-American War, which ended in 1848.

That defeat left Mexico more vulnerable than ever. In 1862 French troops occupied the country. They remained until 1867, when Mexicans regained control of their nation under President Benito Juárez, who backed land reforms to aid poor people in rural areas. Their plight was largely ignored by President Porfirio Díaz, who took office in 1876. Díaz helped Mexico industrialize with foreign investment but stifled democracy, fueling anger that erupted in revolution in 1910.

BENITO JUÁREZ

Benito Juárez, shown at center in this mural, was born a Zapotec Indian in the state of Oaxaca (wah-HAH-kah) in 1806 and became Mexico's first Indian president in 1861. When French troops occupied Mexico City a year later, he fled with his government to the border town known today as Ciudad Juárez. He used armed force and diplomatic pressure to drive the French out and returned as president in 1867. He died in office five years later. Today Juárez is revered in Mexico.

A Decade of Revolution

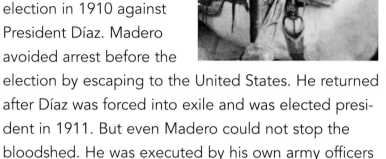

The Mexican Revolution was ignited by Francisco I. Madero, a champion of democracy who ran for election in 1910 against President Díaz. Madero avoided arrest before the election by escaping to the United States. He returned after Díaz was forced into exile and was elected president in 1911. But even Madero could not stop the bloodshed. He was executed by his own army officers in 1913.

◀ Pancho Villa was the eldest child of a poor farmer who died and left him to look after the family. Hailed as a Mexican Robin Hood for robbing the rich and helping the poor, he joined the revolution in 1910.

▼ Emiliano Zapata was born poor and got in trouble at an early age. At 18, he was arrested for organizing a protest by poor farmers against a wealthy landowner.

As the brutal fighting continued, men like Pancho Villa (PAHN-cho VEE-yah) and Emiliano Zapata attacked rich landowners and gave their land to the poor. They fought hard to remove from power officials like Venustiano Carranza, who became president in 1917. When Carranza failed to implement the radical new constitution favored by the revolution's leaders, he too was overthrown. By the time the revolution ended, nearly 1.5 million Mexicans had died and another million had left the country.

A
Colorful
Blend
of
Traditions

URN ANY CORNER in Mexico today and you will likely see evidence of Mexico's rich cultural heritage. Plazas, like Mexico City's Zócalo, still serve as ceremonial centers, just as they did in the days of the Maya, Aztec, and Spanish colonists. Cathedrals are prominent, as they were with Spanish colonists, but they are painted with bright Indian colors. At carnival time, dancers honor creatures once revered by the Maya and the Aztec.

For Mexicans of mixed heritage, the long relationship between the Indians and the Spaniards has finally resulted in something worth celebrating: a culture that harmoniously blends traditions of the Old World and the New.

◀ Worshippers honor the Virgin of Guadalupe, also called Our Lady of Guadalupe, with music and pageantry in the town of Quetzalen.

RURAL & URBAN POPULATION

The population of Mexico has grown rapidly in recent years, topping 100 million in 2004 (see map opposite). At the same time, many people have moved from rural to urban areas.

Today, Mexico City alone is home to nearly one-fifth of the nation's population. But not all Mexicans are on the move or adopting new ways. More than five million people in Mexico speak a native language and may never use Spanish. They are considered Indians, even if they have some Spanish ancestry. Others of Indian heritage have assimilated—adapted to the culture of the Hispanic majority—and speak Spanish. They are considered mestizos even if they have no Spanish ancestry. In the southern states of Oaxaca and Chiapas, unassimilated Indians make up more than one-quarter of the population.

Common Spanish Phrases

Here are a few Spanish words and phrases you might use in Mexico. Give them a try:

¡Hola! (OH-lah)   Hello!

Buenos días   Good day, good morning
(bweh-nohs DEE-ahs)

Por qué? (pohr kay)   Why?

Por favor (pohr fah-VOHR) Please

Madre (MAH-dray)   Mother

Padre (PAH-dray)   Father

¡Gracias! (GRAH-seeus) Thanks!

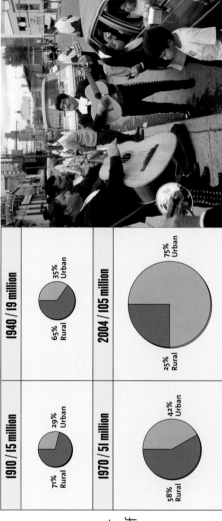

▶ **Mariachi bands play lively and spirited tunes—the "music of the people."**

1910 / 15 million	1940 / 19 million
29% Urban / 71% Rural	35% Urban / 65% Rural

1970 / 51 million	2004 / 105 million
42% Urban / 58% Rural	75% Urban / 25% Rural

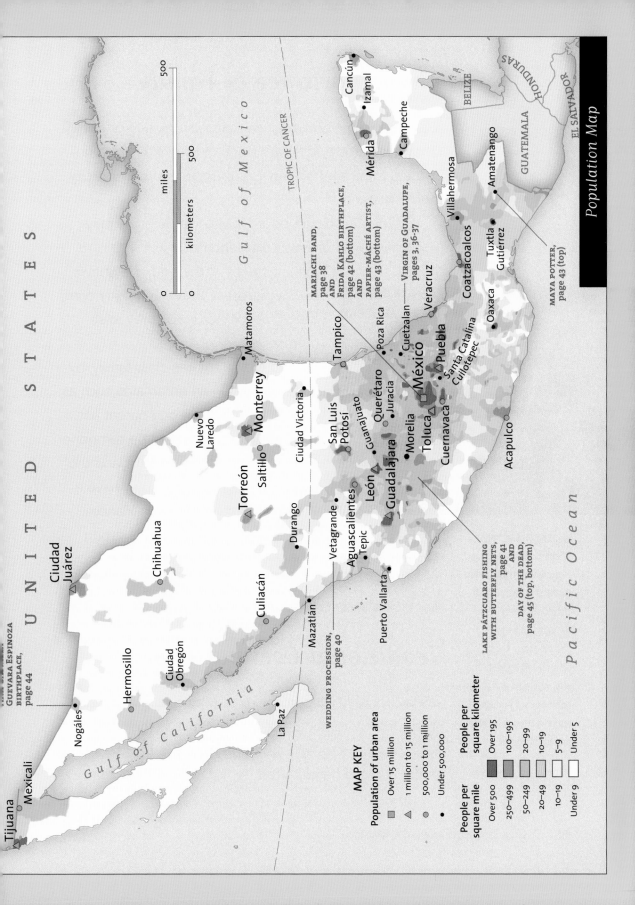

Population Map

MAP KEY

Population of urban area
- ■ Over 15 million
- ▲ 1 million to 15 million
- ● 500,000 to 1 million
- • Under 500,000

People per square mile
	People per square kilometer
■ Over 500	Over 195
■ 250–499	100–195
■ 50–249	20–99
20–49	10–19
10–19	5–9
Under 9	Under 5

GUEVARA ESPINOZA
BIRTHPLACE,
page 44

WEDDING PROCESSION,
page 40

LAKE PÁTZCUARO FISHING
WITH BUTTERFLY NETS,
page 41
AND
DAY OF THE DEAD,
page 45 (top, bottom)

MARIACHI BAND,
page 38
AND
FRIDA KAHLO BIRTHPLACE,
page 42 (bottom)
AND
PAPIER-MÂCHÉ ARTIST,
page 43 (bottom)

VIRGIN OF GUADALUPE,
pages 3, 36-37

MAYA POTTER,
page 43 (top)

UNITED STATES

Tijuana
Mexicali
Nogáles
Ciudad Juárez
Hermosillo
Ciudad Obregón
La Paz
Chihuahua
Culiacán
Mazatlán
Torreón
Saltillo
Durango
Nuevo Laredo
Monterrey
Matamoros
Ciudad Victoria
Puerto Vallarta
Vetagrande
Durango
Tepic
Aguascalientes
San Luis Potosí
Tampico
Guadalajara
León
Guanajuato
Querétaro
Juracia
Morelia
Toluca
México
Santa Catalina Cuilotepec
Cuernavaca
Puebla
Acapulco
Poza Rica
Cuetzalan
Veracruz
Oaxaca
Coatzacoalcos
Villahermosa
Tuxtla Gutiérrez
Amatenango
Campeche
Mérida
Izamal
Cancún

Gulf of California

Pacific Ocean

Gulf of Mexico

TROPIC OF CANCER

BELIZE
GUATEMALA
HONDURAS
EL SALVADOR

miles
500
kilometers
500

0
0
500
500

The Importance of Family

Like people everywhere, Mexicans can be rich or poor. They live in many different kinds of dwellings, from tin-roofed, one-room houses to suburban mansions to city apartments.

Children from the poorest Mexican families may not be allowed to finish elementary school. Their homes may not have electricity. If they do, they have few appliances. They eat mostly corn, beans, and other crops they raise themselves.

The typical middle-class family, by contrast, lives in an urban area such as Mexico City. At least one parent has a good job, and there may be someone hired to help with housework and the children. People in this family have a varied diet and modern appliances.

▲ Friends and family follow Gabriel Hernández and his bride through the streets of their hometown of Vetagrande on their wedding day. Soon Gabriel will be off to the city, where he can get a job that pays enough to support his wife, mother, and six brothers.

One thing all Mexicans have in common is strong family ties. Even an only child will have an extended family of aunts, uncles, cousins, grandparents, and *comadres* and *compadres*—godparents.

Traditional Occupations

Today, roughly 30 percent of all Mexicans make their living from traditional occupations just as their ancestors did centuries ago. Some farm, some fish, some make and sell handcrafted items, such as silver jewelry,

pottery, and embroidered clothing. These traditional workers face an uncertain future. People selling their own handiwork must compete with crafts made in factories. Many traditional farmers use old-fashioned plows and cannot afford fertilizers. Those who live by fishing have to cope with polluted or overfished waters. Sometimes these hardworking people find it difficult to feed their families. But there is some good news. Collectives—groups of workers—have begun to organize to export their wares and sell them abroad, keeping most of the money from the sales for themselves.

Foods from Near & Far

Mexican food is a blend of ingredients from home and abroad. Many items sold in Mexican markets—

▲ Tarascan Indians on Lake Pátzcuaro, southwest of Guadalajara, paddle their canoes in a circle to confine tiny white fish called charales then catch them in butterfly nets.

including corn, beans, tomatoes, chocolate, chili peppers, avocados, and turkeys—are native to the country. Other foods—including wheat, onions, chicken, and cheese—were introduced by the Spanish. Mexican cooks combine these New and Old World ingredients, for example, topping chicken with *molé poblano*, a sauce of chocolate, chilis, and other spices.

▲ Tomatoes grew in Mexico long before the Spanish arrived.

A Gallery of Art

Throughout its history, Mexico has been home to great artists. Long before the Spanish conquest, the Maya and other Indians were painting impressive murals at Bonampak (in the state of Chiapas) and elsewhere. Those early artists also made beautiful sculptures, jewelry, and household goods. When the Spanish

FANTASTIC PICTURES

Frida Kahlo (1907—1954)

Some love her paintings, some think they are weird, but all agree that Frida Kahlo was a fascinating artist with a drama-filled life. Crippled by polio and a near-fatal bus accident, she began painting while bedridden. She married the painter Diego Rivera; their life together was filled with wild romance and furious fighting. Best known for her colorful self-portraits with animals, Frida forged a lively career among artists in Mexico and abroad. Often in severe pain, Frida kept painting to the end of her life.

came, they added their artistic techniques, such as oil painting, to those of the Indians. Modern Mexicans include some of the world's great painters, photographers, sculptors, and muralists. Mexico has also nurtured great writers, including Carlos Fuentes, Nobel-Prize-winner Octavio Paz, and Rosario Castellanos, a poet and novelist.

▲ A Maya potter wearing a traditional embroidered blouse works on a vase at her shop in the state of Chiapas.

▼ A Mexican artist puts the finishing touches on a papier-mâché sculpture of fighting dragons.

Folk Art & Crafts

Millions of tourists come to Mexico every year to view the artistic wonders of its past and admire the work of today's potters, woodworkers, silversmiths, and other artisans. These craft workers combine Indian traditions that go back thousands of years with techniques brought to Mexico by the Spanish to create their unique cultural look. Potters use Spanish pottery wheels to make pots decorated with native designs. Artists use paper, first brought here from Spain, to create papier-mâché sculptures and figurines, many of them inspired by Mexican folklore.

Some of the finest examples of Mexican folk art can be seen in Catholic churches and at Catholic festivals. Spaniards introduced the religion, but Indians here gave Catholicism a bright new look by crafting dazzling religious objects in native style

▲ Runner Ana Gabriela Guevara Espinoza holds the Mexican flag aloft at the world championships in Edmonton, Canada, in 2001.

and painting churches in the vivid colors their ancestors once used to decorate ancient temples.

A Passion for Sports

Mexicans take sports seriously. In a country where losers in ritual ball games were put to death during Maya times, people still compete as if their lives depended on it. The risks are real for matadors, who are sometimes gored by bulls. Other sports figures work just as hard. Mexicans imported baseball from the U.S., but they originated the rodeo where Mexican cowboys, called *charros*, compete with each other at roping calves or riding wild bulls.

Mexico also fields a team at the Olympics. In 2004, Ana Gabriela Guevara Espinoza entered the 400-meter race as the world record holder and won the silver medal.

Celebrating Death & Renewal

On the first two days of November, Mexicans celebrate with gifts, flowers, and dances something many people in other

NATIONAL HOLIDAYS

Official holidays include religious celebrations such as Easter (Pascua) and Christmas (Navidad). Columbus Day is known as the Day of the Race—the mixed race that resulted from intermarriage between the Spaniards and the native peoples.

January 1
New Year's Day

February 5
Constitution Day

March 21
Benito Juárez Day

March/April
Good Friday and Pascua (Easter) Week

May 1
Labor Day (International Worker's Day)

May 5
Cinco de Mayo (celebrates a victory over the French)

September 16
Independence Day

October 12
Día de la Raza (Columbus Day)

November 1 & 2
Day of the Dead

November 20
Revolution Day

December 12
Our Lady of Guadalupe Day

December 25
Navidad (Christmas)

lands would rather not think about—death. During this holiday, known as the Day of the Dead, children wear skeleton costumes and eat small skulls made of sugar. People visit the graves of their loved ones and leave food and other presents. The festival coincides with the Catholic holidays of All Saints' Day (November 1) and All Souls' Day (November 2), but it owes much to ancient beliefs and rituals that Indians observed. Long before Christianity arrived here, people in Mexico believed that offerings from the living helped spirits reach the next world and enter a new existence. Like many holidays, the celebration is a way for people to honor the struggles and sacrifices of past generations.

▲ Traditionally, Mexicans honor the souls of children on November 1 and the souls of adults on November 2.

▼ A puppet in a skeleton costume for the Day of the Dead

Emerging Mexico

WHEN MEXICO'S PRESIDENT stands before the National Palace in Zócalo square on Independence Day and recalls Miguel Hidalgo y Costilla's fiery speech that ignited the War for Independence in 1810, he honors all the fallen heroes who died fighting for freedom in Mexico.

But even today, freedom has not brought Mexico all the benefits the nation's founders had anticipated. This is an emerging country, with great problems and great potential. Mexico has not yet achieved widespread prosperity or consistently good government. But those goals, fought for in the decade-long revolution that ended back in 1920, are within reach.

◀ **Workers raise their fists in protest during a rally at the Zócalo in 1996.**

POLITICS AS USUAL

Mexico has 31 states, each with its own capital, and a Federal District with a national capital in Mexico City (see political map on the opposite page). Some large states such as Baja California have subdivided. Others like Sonora and Chihuahua are larger than many nations and have long borders with the U.S. that are mostly unpatrolled.

Under the current constitution, states have less power than they did when the United Mexican States was founded in 1824. The government controls the oil industry, develops resorts for tourism, and offers tax breaks to those operating factories called maquiladoras along the Mexican-American border. Many Mexicans go to border cities like Tijuana to work in maquiladoras. Others simply pass through— legally or illegally—on their way to the U.S. in pursuit of higher wages and better living conditions.

Trading Partners

Mexico trades with nations across the globe, sending petroleum and petroleum products, coffee, vegetables, cotton, fruit, silver, and machine parts abroad, and importing industrial and farm machinery and electrical equipment.

Country	Percent Mexico exports
United States	87.6%
Canada	1.8%
Spain	1.1%
All others combined 8%	

Country	Percent Mexico imports
United States	53.7%
Japan	7%
China	5.1%
All others combined 27%	

▼ A woman at a maquiladora in Matamoros turns out sweatshirts at a fast clip.

Political Map

MAP KEY

⊛ National capital
◉ State capital
• Other city
● Paired U.S. border city
SINALOA Mexican state name

mi 0 200
km 0 200

ILLEGAL IMMIGRATION, page 55

MAQUILADORA FACTORY, page 48

PROTEST AT THE ZÓCALO, pages 3, 46-47
AND
STOCK EXCHANGE, page 52

TOURISM, page 56

OFFSHORE OIL PLATFORMS, page 54

RANCH HANDS AT WORK, page 51

MOON RISE AT LAND'S END, page 57

Gulf of Mexico

Pacific Ocean

Gulf of California

TROPIC OF CANCER

UNITED STATES

ARIZONA
NEW MEXICO
TEXAS
LOUISIANA
MISS.
ALABAMA
FLA.

MEXICO

BAJA CALIFORNIA
BAJA CALIFORNIA SUR
SONORA
CHIHUAHUA
SINALOA
DURANGO
COAHUILA
NUEVO LEÓN
TAMAULIPAS
ZACATECAS
NAYARIT
JALISCO
AGUASCALIENTES
SAN LUIS POTOSÍ
GUANAJUATO
QUERÉTARO
HIDALGO
COLIMA
MICHOACÁN
MEXICO
FEDERAL DISTRICT
TLAXCALA
PUEBLA
MORELOS
GUERRERO
VERACRUZ
OAXACA
TABASCO
CHIAPAS
CAMPECHE
YUCATÁN
QUINTANA ROO

GUATEMALA
BELIZE
HONDURAS
EL SALVADOR

Chula Vista
Tijuana
Mexicali
Calexico
Nogales
Nogales
Douglas
Agua Prieta
Cananea
Hermosillo
El Paso
Ciudad Juárez
Chihuahua
Ciudad Acuña
Del Rio
Eagle Pass
Piedras Negras
Nuevo Laredo
Laredo
Reynosa
McAllen
Brownsville
Matamoros
Monterrey
Saltillo
Torreón
Durango
Ciudad Victoria
Culiacán
Tepic
La Paz
Cabo San Lucas
Puerto Vallarta
Guadalajara
Aguascalientes
Zacatecas
San Luis Potosí
León
Guanajuato
Querétaro
Colima
Morelia
Toluca
Taxco
Chilpancingo
Acapulco
Tampico
Poza Rica
Pachuca
MÉXICO
Tlaxcala
Puebla
Cuernavaca
Jalapa
Veracruz
Oaxaca
Villahermosa
Tuxtla Gutiérrez
Campeche
Mérida
Chetumal
Cancún Island

115°W 110°W 105°W 100°W 95°W 90°W
30°N 25°N 20°N 15°N

Mexican Politics since the Revolution

When the revolution ended in 1920, most Mexicans backed the party that would become what is known today as the PRI (Party of Revolutionary Institutions). The PRI promised to peacefully pursue the revolution's goals, but some of its leaders were more interested in power than in democracy.

Party founder Plutarco Elías Calles ran the government until 1934, when Lázaro Cárdenas, the candidate Calles backed for president, redistributed almost 50 million acres of land to poor Mexicans. Cárdenas also nationalized oil companies in Mexico, many of them American owned.

By 1940, Mexico's ruling party was revolutionary in name only. Mexico was rapidly industrializing. Party

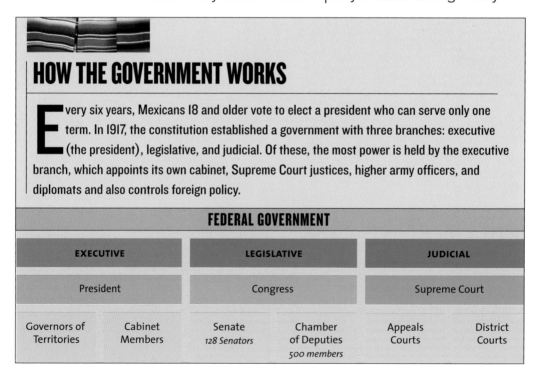

HOW THE GOVERNMENT WORKS

Every six years, Mexicans 18 and older vote to elect a president who can serve only one term. In 1917, the constitution established a government with three branches: executive (the president), legislative, and judicial. Of these, the most power is held by the executive branch, which appoints its own cabinet, Supreme Court justices, higher army officers, and diplomats and also controls foreign policy.

FEDERAL GOVERNMENT

EXECUTIVE		LEGISLATIVE		JUDICIAL	
President		Congress		Supreme Court	
Governors of Territories	Cabinet Members	Senate *128 Senators*	Chamber of Deputies *500 members*	Appeals Courts	District Courts

leaders controlled labor unions and workers' wages. Economic growth, combined with government health care and housing programs, led to a gradual increase in Mexico's standard of living.

Changing Times

Twenty years later, Mexicans too young to remember the revolution were shocked when the government began to use army units as well as police to crush political protests. In 1968, scores of demonstrators were killed in Mexico City shortly before Mexico hosted the Summer Olympics. Even people who disagreed with the protesters blamed party leaders for using excessive force and tolerating police brutality.

▲ With no truck to ease his task, a ranch hand in Chiapas carries a stray calf over his shoulders. Hardships like these, faced by farmers and laborers in Chiapas, one of Mexico's poorest states, led to the Zapatista uprising in 1994.

Economic troubles made things worse for Mexico's ruling party. Falling oil prices left the government deeply in debt. By late 1987, the peso was worth less than one-twentieth of a U.S. cent. The party suffered another blow in 1994 when rebels calling themselves Zapatistas rose up in rural Chiapas. Some denounced the PRI for abandoning its promise of a better life for the poor in rural areas like Chiapas. Others faulted the party for failing to preserve law and order. In 2000, the PRI's control came to an end with the victory of Vicente Fox, candidate of the National Action Party (PAN).

▲ These traders on the stock exchange in Mexico City serve as links between Mexican businesses and the global economy.

A MODERN REVOLUTION

In January 1994, masked gunmen swarmed across Chiapas, a state rich in agriculture and oil reserves, though many of its people are very poor. In honor of revolutionary leader Emiliano Zapata, they called themselves the Zapatista Army of National Liberation. Most of their demands were simple—the right to own land, better schools, health care, and self-government. Today, the Zapatistas have founded 32 towns with independent town councils and services. Their goals have expanded to include better conditions for all native people—both inside and outside Chiapas.

Finding a Place in the Global Economy

The biggest changes facing Mexicans today are not political but economic. Mexico's business is now the world's business and must respond to pressures from global consumers, producers, and international investors. Deals made on the stock exchange in Mexico City are tied to deals in New York, Tokyo, and other distant financial centers.

The Mexican economy has long depended heavily on natural resources such as silver, copper, and oil. Mexico is still the world's leading producer of silver. Its oil companies are government owned, but that does not protect Mexico from global economic pressures. If demand drops and prices fall, companies may have to cut production and lay off workers unless the government can afford to subsidize the companies.

Workers in other nations have faced similar pressures in recent decades. Governments that once tried to protect industries by subsidizing them or placing tariffs (taxes) on imported goods have moved toward free trade. Mexico embraced free trade in 1994 when it joined the U.S. and Canada in NAFTA (the North

INDUSTRY & MINING

This map shows the locations of some industrial and mining operations in Mexico. Industrial production accounts for 25 percent of Mexico's economy.

Major Mines

Au Gold	Pb Lead
Ag Silver	Mn Manganese
Cu Copper	S Sulfur
F Fluorite	Zn Zinc
Fe Iron ore	

- ✹ Manufacturing center
- ▲ Natural gas
- ⚭ Petroleum
- Cu Refinery
- ○ Salt
- Steel Steel manufacturing

American Free Trade Agreement). The agreement called for the gradual elimination of tariffs on most products traded between the three countries. Since then, Mexico has reached free trade agreements with other countries.

The Future of Free Trade

Only time will tell if free trade will bring long-term benefits to Mexico. Labor is a lot cheaper in Mexico than in the U.S. An American worker earns nearly as much in an hour as a Mexican worker doing the same task earns in a day. That means Mexican factories can produce goods at lower cost than American factories and sell them in the U.S. at lower prices. Mexican workers face increasing competition, however, from

▼ Workers tend an oil rig in the Gulf of Mexico off Campeche. A government-owned company called Pemex controls the production of oil, one of Mexico's leading exports.

laborers in Asia and Central America who produce goods for even less. That competition makes it difficult for Mexican workers to form unions and bargain for higher wages.

Life on the Border: Rewards and Risks

Since the 1990s, many poor families from rural Mexico have looked to border cities such as Ciudad Juárez, Matamoros, and Tijuana, where maquiladoras (factories) use Mexican workers to produce goods for export, mainly to the U.S. The pay is low by American standards but good enough by Mexican standards to attract thousands of opportunity seekers whose new lives will have rewards as well as risks.

Cities like Ciudad Juárez are typically overcrowded. Families moving there may find themselves forced to live in cramped dwellings with no electricity and no running water. Their days at the factory are long, and the hours they work are grueling. Eventually, many maquiladora workers will cross into the United States for better pay and better living conditions.

ILLEGAL IMMIGRATION

Every year, many Mexicans risk arrest, injury, or death by crossing into the U.S. illegally. Some, like this family, wade across the Rio Grande. Others cross the desert on foot at night, hide in trucks, or cram into tight spaces to avoid detection. Today, more than five million Mexicans are thought to be working in the U.S. illegally. Mexicans living in the U.S. send an estimated 14 billion dollars to their families in Mexico each year.

▲ A Mexican family crosses the Rio Grande from Matamoros to Brownsville, Texas.

Tourism: It's Big Business

Beginning in the late 1960s, Mexico's government began using some of its oil profits to develop new areas for tourism. It built roads, airports, and other facilities and encouraged private investors to put up hotels and restaurants. The most successful of those projects was Cancún, whose glitzy beachfront lured hordes of sun worshippers to the nearby Yucatán coast. By the 1990s, it was Mexico's most popular tourist destination, outdrawing Mexico City.

▼ Cancún has been growing like wildfire since the 1970s and now, despite setbacks such as hurricanes, attracts nearly one and a half million tourists a year.

Today, Mexico's annual income from tourism exceeds ten billion dollars. As tourists venture out from resorts such as Cancún to visit Maya ruins, coastal wetlands, and other sites of natural or historical interest, more people are beginning to share in the economic benefits. But tourism has a benefit that cannot be measured in pesos, dollars, or any other currency. It brings foreigners in touch with Mexico and leaves them with a deeper appreciation for this remarkable country.

▼ The government-planned resort at Cabo San Lucas on the southern tip of Baja California blends in nicely with its surroundings.

Index

Boldface indicates illustrations.

Credits

Picture Credits

Front Cover—Spine: Philip Coblentz/PictureQuest; Top: Robert Frerck/Stone/Getty Images; Low far left: Gavin Hellier/Robert Harding World Imagery/Getty Images; Low left: Robert Frerck/Stone/Getty Images; Low right: Phil Schermeister/NG Image Collection; Low far right: Alyx Kellington/Index Stock Imagery.

Interior—Corbis: Bettmann: 35 up, 35 lo, 42 lo right; Kenneth Dannemiller: 52 up; Randy Farris: 2-3, 24-25; Danny Lehman: 3 right, 46-47; George D. Lepp: 22 lo; Reuters: K. Lamarque: 44 up; Getty Images: 2 right, 16-17, 42 up; Jupiter Images: Philip Coblentz: spine, 2up, 4, 12lo, 14 up left, 22up, 33up, 34 up, 42 lo left, 44 lo, 50, 52 lo, 53 up, 55up, 58, 59, 60, 62, 64; NG Image Collection: 14 lo, 26, 28, 30 up, 30 lo; Sissie Brimberg: 43 lo; Lee Bolton: 31; Richard Alexander Cooke III: 15; Bruce Dale: 11; Stuart Franklin: 13, 39, 54; Kenneth Garrett: 3 left, 23 up, 29, 36-37; George Grall: 20 up, 23 lo; Annie Griffiths: 21; David Alan Harvey: 1, 40, 41, 45 up, 57; Bill Hatcher: 20 lo; Otis Imboden: 43 up; Sarah Leen: 2 left, 6-7; Pierre Mion: 14 up right; Joel Sartore: 5, 10, 48, 55 lo; Phil Schermeister: 32; Maria Stenzel: 12 up; Tomasz Tomaszewski: 51, 56; Odyssey Productions: Robert Frerck (painting by Orozco): 34 lo; Picturequest: 45 lo; SeaPics.com: Amar Guillen: 18

For more information, please call 1-800-NGS-LINE (647-5463) or write to the following address:

NATIONAL GEOGRAPHIC SOCIETY
1145 17th Street N.W.
Washington, D.C. 20036-4688 U.S.A.

Visit the Society's Web site at www.nationalgeographic.com

Library of Congress Cataloging-in-Publication Data available on request
Hardcover ISBN-10: 0-7922-7629-9
Hardcover ISBN-13: 978-0-7922-7629-6
Library Edition ISBN-10: 0-7922-7669-8
Library Edition ISBN-13: 978-0-7922-7669-2

Printed in Belgium

Book design by Jim Hiscott.
The body text is set in Avenir; Knockout.
The display text is set in Matrix Script.

Front Cover—Top: Lake Patzcuaro; Low far left: Chichen Itza, Yucatan; Low left: Mexico City; Low right: Magdalena; Low far right: Coyoacan

Page 1—Cacti frame a view of the hillside town of Guanajuato, in central Mexico; Icon image on spine, Contents page, and throughout: Beautiful blankets on display outside a Mexican shop.

Produced through the worldwide resources of the National Geographic Society

John M. Fahey, Jr., *President and Chief Executive Officer;* Gilbert M. Grosvenor, *Chairman of the Board;* Nina D. Hoffman, *Executive Vice President, President of Books and Education Publishing Group*

Prepared by National Geographic Children's Books and Education Publishing Group

Stephen Mico, *Executive Vice President and Publisher, Children's Books and Education Publishing Group*
Bea Jackson, *Design Director, Children's Books and Education Publishing Group*
Margaret Sidlosky, *Illustrations Director, Children's Books and Education Publishing Group*

Staff for this Book

Nancy Laties Feresten, *Vice President, Editor-in-Chief of Children's Books*
Virginia Koeth, *Project Editor*
Jim Hiscott, *Art Director*
National Geographic Image Sales, Lori Epstein, *Illustrations Editors*
Carl Mehler, *Director of Maps*
Priyanka Lamichhane, *Editorial Assistant*
Margie Towery, *Indexer*
Rebecca Hinds, *Managing Editor*
R. Gary Colbert, *Production Director*
Lewis R. Bassford, *Production Manager*
Vincent P. Ryan, Maryclare Tracy, *Manufacturing Managers*

About the Author

BETH SLONE GRUBER is a graduate of the New York University School of Journalism. She has worked in children's publishing for almost 20 years as an author, editor, and reviewer of books for young readers. She has written a second book on the National Geographic list titled *National Geographic Investigates: Ancient Inca.* She lives in New York City.

About the Consultants

DR. GARY S. ELBOW is a professor of geography and associate dean of the Honors College at Texas Tech University. He is a specialist in Latin American geography who has lived or traveled in most of the countries of the region. Dr.Elbow has made many trips to Mexico and knows the country well. At Texas Tech he teaches a course on the North American Free Trade Agreement.

DR. JORGE ZAMORA is an assistant professor of Spanish at Texas Tech University, where he teaches Business Spanish and Mexican Literature. Born and raised in Mexico City, he received his law degree from the National University of Mexico in 1984. His Ph. D. in Spanish from Texas Tech was awarded in 1999.